Delegating

Time-saving books that teach specific skills to busy people, focusing on what really matters; the things that make a difference – the *essentials*.

Other books in the series include:

Hiring People

The Ultimate Business Plan

Accounting for the Small Business

Making the Most of Your Time

Develop a Winning Market Plan

Coaching People

Leading Teams

Making Meetings Work

The 80/20 Management Rule

Solving Problems

Writing Business E-mails

Delegating

Julie-Ann Amos

ESSENTIALS

Published in 2001 by
How To Books Ltd, 3 Newtec Place,
Magdalen Road, Oxford OX4 1RE, United Kingdom
Tel: (01865) 793806   Fax: (01865) 248780
email: info@howtobooks.co.uk
www.howtobooks.co.uk

British Library Cataloguing in Publication Data
A catalogue record for this book is available from
the British Library

Edited by Diana Brueton
Cover design by Shireen Nathoo Design, London
Produced for How To Books by Deer Park Productions
Designed and typeset by Shireen Nathoo Design, London
Printed and bound in Great Britain by Bell & Bain Ltd., Glasgow

NOTE: The material contained in this book is set out in good faith for
general guidance and no liability can be accepted for loss or expense
incurred as a result of relying in particular circumstances on statements
made in the book. The laws and regulations are complex and liable to
change, and readers should check the current position with the relevant
authorities before making personal arrangements.

ESSENTIALS *is an imprint of*
How To Books

Contents

Preface

Giving work to other people isn't delegation. It's giving out work. Delegation means actually giving someone else control of something that is *part of your job*.

It isn't easy. If it were as easy as giving someone a task and letting them get on with it, delegation would be problem-free. But you have to delegate the right tasks, to the right people, in a way that works for both them and you. You have to keep responsibility for the work, but give them the authority to get on with it. Then you have to keep an eye on them in case they struggle or make mistakes, without being overbearing or watching them like a hawk.

Getting the balance right with delegation can be very tricky. This book will help you see how best to delegate in your own job, to maximise the benefits to you and the others involved.

Julie-Ann Amos

1 Introduction

Delegation is the single most effective tool you have at your disposal, done properly. It frees up your time to do other things, and motivates and develops others. Everybody wins!

In this chapter, four things that really matter:

~ **Assess your delegation**
~ **Understand delegation's advantages**
~ **Beware of potential problems**
~ **Knowing when to delegate**

Delegation is something that people often view as a formal management technique. But really, it is something that people do every day. Whenever you ask someone to do something for you, and hand over the control of the task, you are delegating – in a way.

But what we really mean by delegation at work is giving someone else part of your job. It's giving someone something to do that you should be doing. So it's inherently risky:

you lose complete control over something you are responsible for, and that can be a real worry.

There are many other reasons why people don't delegate, apart from concern over the results. They may not know how, or it may just never have occurred to them. They may be hesitant to add to the workload of others.*

Is this you?

I can't delegate – I don't have the time. • It's a great idea in theory, but you should see the idiots I've got working for me! • I love delegating! Get rid of your work to others so you can get out and about more. That's got to bring your stress levels down, hasn't it? • The last time I delegated something to Anna she got very affronted – she really resented doing my work for me. I don't want to upset anyone again. • Well, I tried it, but it took so long checking up on everyone, I might as well have done it myself, in half the time! • I hate delegating. It's just too much trouble – more than it's worth!

* By not delegating we miss out on the incredible efficiency and effectiveness you can create in a team.

Assess your delegation

Delegation skills are something that people often think they have, when they haven't. Or, people don't think they know how to delegate but they actually do. So how well do you delegate at the moment? A lot of people don't even think about it, let alone try to find out! *

How well do you delegate?

Here is a simple test to help you judge how well you delegate at present. Simply answer whether you agree or disagree with each statement. Then score your answers from the table listed at the end of the test. This will give you a rough feeling for how well you are delegating at present.

* Most people are never taught how to delegate. They just get on with it and hope for the best. So it's hardly surprising that a lot of people are awful delegators!

1   Can the people working with you act fully in your absence if necessary?

2   Is the majority of your work composed of tasks that only you can do?

3   Do you have the time to talk to people about any work issues they may have for

any length of time?

4   Are you frequently interrupted by people asking you for decisions or guidance so that they can get on with their own work?

5   Are you meeting all your deadlines without needing to do very long hours?

6   Do people around you sometimes feel you dump work on them?

7   If you were hospitalised tomorrow, would anyone know how to pick up your work and get it done?

8   Do you frequently over-rule decisions that other people have made?

9   Do you often re-do tasks you have given to others?

10   Do you have problems getting people to take responsibility for a job or task?

11   Do you ever find that people let you down and don't meet the deadlines you set them?

12 Do people often ask you if you need any help or if there is anything they can do for you?

13 Do people look interested and pleased when you approach them about taking on a task?

14 Do you have the time to plan your work and manage your own workload?

15 Do you invest time in training others?

16 Do you ever do jobs that someone else could do more quickly and easily?

17 Do you have the time to consider your work, and how things such as systems and processes could be improved?

18 Are you good at setting objectives and letting people get on with the task?

19 Do you do work that is junior or routine; that someone else on a lower salary could handle?

20 Does everyone in your team have an equal workload?

21   Do you spend a lot of time checking up on other people's progress?

22   Are your standards pretty much equal to those of people around you?

23   Are people happy to admit it to you when they have made a mistake?

24   Do you find that people follow your instructions properly?

Scoring

Score points as shown. If you really can't decide, and the answer is sometimes yes, sometimes no, score 2 points.

What does it mean?

Basically, the higher your score, the worse you are at delegating, or the more you should think about increasing your delegation.

Question	Points for agree	Points for disagree
1	1	3
2	3	1
3	1	3
4	3	1
5	1	3
6	3	1
7	1	3
8	3	1
9	3	1
10	3	1
11	3	1
12	3	1
13	1	3
14	1	3
15	1	3
16	3	1
17	1	3
18	1	3
19	3	1
20	1	3
21	3	1
22	1	3
23	1	3
24	1	3

24-30 points

Your delegation is pretty good! If you answered honestly, you shouldn't have too many problems with your delegation. Hopefully, though, you will gain at least a few pointers from this book.

31-50 points

Your delegation is a little hit and miss. Sometimes it works out, but a lot of the time it doesn't. You need to sharpen your delegation skills, and a little effort could reap huge rewards.

51-72 points

Oh dear! Your delegation skills are pretty weak at present, but at least you have made a positive step by reading this book! You need to put some time and effort into your delegating, in order to make you more skilful. It's very worthwhile in the long term.

Understand delegation's advantages

Delegation has an enormous number of advantages. There are obvious advantages for you, but consider the advantages for the people you delegate to, and your organisation as a whole. *

Advantages for you

~ You will have more time.

~ You have freedom to concentrate on other things – planning, organising, motivating – even your own work!

~ You are less likely to be or become stressed and/or burnt out.

~ Your output is protected in the event of your unforeseen absence for any length of time.

~ You gain respect from your staff.

~ You are relieved of routine and unimportant tasks.

* Don't keep a dog and bark yourself! Let people do what they're capable of doing.

~ It is easier to meet deadlines and get more done.

~ You get satisfaction from seeing others progress.

~ You build a more integrated team.

Advantages for the person to whom you delegate

~ They are developed: they get to use their existing skills to the full, and learn new ones as well.

~ They feel involved, and therefore happier in their work.

~ They save time – they can act without having to wait for your decision.

~ They have more responsibility.

~ A challenge is good for them.

~ Their confidence and self-esteem improve – which usually increases motivation.

Advantages for your organisation

~ Morale is improved.

~ Decisions can often be better, as they are being made by people closer to the action.

~ Work continues with minimum disruption whilst you are on holiday, off sick, etc.

~ Improved teamwork.

~ More work gets done!

~ Succession planning and promotion are prepared for.

~ There is a more trusting, responsible culture.

~ Money is saved by tasks being done at the right level – productivity and efficiency increase.

Beware of potential problems

So if delegation has so many advantages, why don't people practise it more often? Basically, because a lot of people are just afraid of things going wrong. Fear of upsetting a stable working environment can make many managers avoid starting to delegate.

There are many potential problems, so it pays to know about them before you start handing out the work! *

Feeling threatened

There is often a very real fear that if other people know how to do your job, you won't be needed any more. Everyone wants to be valued, and how can you be if you are doing something that anyone else could do?

Solution

Delegating without being aware of some of the potential problems is a recipe for disaster.

You don't let people do everything, just parts of your job. Giving someone the ability to do all your work is called training a replacement, and in some circumstances this might be a wise course of action for you. But setting this aside, you can actually give away tasks that you do on a regular basis, and still keep some work for yourself. Nobody is saying you have to give away all the most favourite parts of your job – you can choose what to delegate!

Loss of control

You may fear loss of control, and so don't delegate as often as you could. You may even do everything yourself.

Solution

Make the person's limits of authority clear, and check on them as and when it's necessary – if only for your own peace of mind!

Loss of quality

You may fear that standards will decline – that no one could do that particular task quite as well as you can.

Solution

Accept that at first, this is true. You probably can do the job better than anyone else. But people do learn, and with time and a little help they will eventually be able to do the task to your standard, without you doing anything at all. Just think of the time you could save.

Fear of constant interruptions

It's true that some people do keep checking for reassurance – reassuring themselves that they are doing things right all the time. This can seem more trouble than it's worth, as it can be a source of constant interruptions to you. But it's usually a passing phase, which decreases or even stops once they are more confident.

Solution

Give praise and feedback. Bolster their self-confidence. Brief them properly in the first place, and encourage management by exception – this is where they only come to you if something out of the ordinary occurs. As a last resort, and if you know they don't really need help, just reassurance, tell them you are too busy right now, and ask that they catch you later. This effectively forces them to stand on their own two feet, and it's surprising how often people will just get on with the job if you're not always available to go to.

People may feel 'put upon'

This usually happens when your delegation is poor, so you can prevent it happening in the first place.

Solution

Spread out the delegation so that no one person gets too much directed at them – no matter how good they are! If one person is better than others, delegate to the others so they learn to be as capable. Brief people properly so that they know why you're delegating to them and what benefit, if any, there is in the task for them.

Fear of being overtaken

You may fear that someone else might do the job even better than you can! This is called insecurity. If they can do it better than you, why is that a problem?

Solution

Think about this. If someone else can do the job better than you, they should be doing it, not you! That's called efficiency – getting the best person to do each task. *

Lack of time

You may think you don't have the time to train someone or brief them so that they can do the job. This is a very common barrier to delegation. You need to invest time now, to save time later.

Solution

If you don't make some time, you will always be as short of time as you are now – nothing will ever change. Tasks that are repetitive, as opposed to 'one-offs' will pay you back many fold after your initial investment of time in training someone.

People are too busy

You may be hesitant to delegate because others already seem busy without adding more to their workload.

* *Let people do what they're good at, and you get on with whatever it is that you're best at!*

Solution

What are people busy doing? Are they all doing work that really needs doing, or are some involved in 'nice to do' but unimportant tasks?   The idea is to allocate work more efficiently, and give everyone better tasks, not just dish out more volume of work. Plus, being considerate to others can mean being inconsiderate to yourself. Lighten your load and spread things around a little.

The work is yours

There is often a belief that because something is your job, or a task was given to you, only you can do it, or should do it. *

Solution

Remember, the desired result is to get the job done. Unless specifically told you were to do it yourself, you can delegate it to get it done.

* Sometimes in life you have to give up doing things and let other people have a go. Otherwise, they never progress – and neither do you, because you'll never have the time!

Knowing when to delegate

Here are some good guidelines for deciding when to delegate – and when not to!

Delegate when:

~ You have more work than you can manage.

~ You have insufficient time for priority work.

~ You want to develop someone.

~ Someone else can do the job perfectly well.

~ Someone needs a boost of motivation.

~ Someone has a particular interest in a task or project.

~ Tasks are time-consuming but not important.

~ You don't want to do the task (but keep this to yourself, or people may feel they're being dumped on!).

Do not delegate when:

~ You would be delegating to someone unable to cope with the task (for obvious reasons).

~ You would be delegating to someone overqualified to do the task (as this is likely to result in them feeling dumped on). *

~ The task is a large or unsolved problem or issue – a hot potato (as this is unfair).

~ The task involves dealing with highly confidential matters (unless you know they can be trusted, and the confidentiality is not regarding their colleagues).

~ The task requires your individual skill or experience.

~ Others are overloaded already.

~ Tasks are so critical that failure would be devastating (this can ruin someone's confidence if they get it wrong, and they are more likely to fail if they are very

* Delegating is not another word for dumping.

anxious about getting it right).

~ Someone is extremely nervous and concerned about the task (because failure can totally demotivate them and strip away all their confidence).

~ A task has been delegated to you specifically by someone else, unless you check with them first (because you never know whether the person had specific reasons of which you are unaware for delegating it to you).

Summary points

★ Don't just hand work out and assume you're a good delegator. Delegation is a skill that can and should be developed.

★ Understand the importance of delegation as a management tool – it is the single most effective thing in developing an efficient working team.

★ Think about why you are reluctant to delegate certain tasks. Is this sensible?

★ Only delegate things that should be delegated. Don't just hand out work willy-nilly and expect good results – or people will come to dread you delegating to them.

2 Planning

You can't just go through your in-tray and start dishing out work to others. You need to plan things properly to delegate effectively.

In this chapter, five things that really matter:

~ **Establish tasks**

~ **Set parameters**

~ **Identify candidates**

~ **Planning**

~ **Responsibility, accountability and authority**

Planning is essential to good, effective delegation. Obviously quick, routine tasks such as phone calls and paperwork can be delegated without a great deal of forethought. But tasks and projects with more depth need to be planned.

Inadequate planning can leave the person being delegated to being overwhelmed, unclear about the objectives, and distressed at the lack of support they feel. It can do the precise opposite of motivating them. It can also leave you with an end result far removed from what you had wanted.

Proper planning means that people will see delegation as motivating, expanding their skills and abilities, and developing their work experience. They will feel they are progressing, and most people like to learn new things – it's stimulating.

Planning doesn't have to be elaborate, just organised. *

Is this you?

By the time I've planned, made the arrangements and delegated, I might as well have done the job myself! • Planning and organising removes people's ability to learn by trial and error. Let's face it, people like a voyage of discovery now and then. • People just get bored when I try to brief them. They prefer to get on with it. • Won't people think I'm silly, telling them how to do everything? • Delegation's about learning how to stand on your own feet. So why do I need to plan things for them?

* Follow some basic principles of delegation and you won't go far wrong.

Establish tasks

The first thing you need to do is to establish exactly what task or tasks you are going to delegate. *

This is actually far easier said than done, because defining exactly where one task ends and another begins can be an interesting and surprising exercise.

Sometimes it can be better to delegate a group of tasks together, so an overall process is delegated. At other times you need to think about delegating just one specific task until you are confident in the person's abilities.

Assess and think

~ Assess your workload.

~ Identify what tasks specifically require you to do them, rather than anyone else.

~ Everything else is potentially work to be delegated.

* Deciding what to delegate can actually be quite enlightening! It can show up all sorts of tasks which aren't necessary or productive.

Identify the easy options

~ Identify tasks that could be done by someone else with no training or briefing.

~ Delegate them!

Establish training needs

~ Identify what could be delegated after giving some training or coaching to someone.

~ Decide what training would be necessary.

~ Is it feasable?

Specify partial projects

~ Identify tasks which can be delegated in part, e.g. parts of large projects.

Give consideration to the whole hog

~ Identify tasks that no-one should be doing.

~ Check if these really are a complete waste of time; because if so, they need to be stopped as soon as possible.

~ Negotiate with the appropriate person to discontinue them (don't just stop, as you may not know whether or not the task is really needed elsewhere in the organisation).

~ Alternatively, you may think about outsourcing these tasks.

Set parameters

Once you have established the task(s) to be delegated, you need to set the parameters. This means deciding to what extent you will delegate the job. There are three main degrees of delegation:

~ Delegating a small element of a task or project.

~ Partial delegation – delegating a task or project but keeping overall responsibility yourself, so that the person reports back to you regularly for instructions.

~ Delegating the whole task or project.

In some ways, there is also a fourth type. We often hear the word abdication, which is where you dump a task or project on someone with no briefing, advice or support.

~ This is abdicating all responsibility for success or failure to the other person.

~ It makes people feel dumped on, and causes poor motivation.

Advantages of whole task delegation

~ Basically, the more of the task you delegate, the better it is for the other person.

~ They will get to see their work as a coherent whole, which is always far more satisfying.

~ Their use of their own initiative is increased

~ Confusion is minimised.

~ Unnecessary and inefficient co-ordination time is saved.

Advantages of partial delegation

~ At first, or if one or other of you is unsure of their abilities, delegate a subtask and not the whole, major task.

~ You can always work up to delegating the whole thing at a later date.

~ Confidence is maintained, as they know they have only part of the task at stake if they make a mistake.

~ You yourself can be more confident, as the consequences of them making a mistake are less serious.

~ You can delegate to new staff, people with no experience, and those unused to responsibility.

Parameters for the manager

There are four golden rules for delegation which you should regard as the parameters for any delegation you do.

~ **Never take the task back** – at least, not if you can possibly help it. It increases your workload, and makes the person concerned feel stupid and humiliated. They will also probably find it hard to pick themselves up and continue with their work afterwards.

~ **Never make changes to the task** – this is hard if the task does evolve, and isn't fixed. But more than one or two minor changes make it very hard for the person doing the task. Changes make people frustrated, and they may lose their motivation and interest. *

~ **Never ever re-delegate to someone else** – this is not just humiliating to the person, it's a public announcement of their incapability compared to the other who has now been given the task. It will almost always cause lack of confidence, humiliation, anger or resentment. Either way, you have quite possibly ruined the relationship between you and them, plus between them and the other person now taking over the task.

* No-one likes it when the goalposts are moved.

~ **Never give more than one person the same task** – it may be tempting to evaluate people against each other, but far from being a healthy competition, people will usually see you as devious and manipulative. If they find out they are both working on the same task they may not bother to do the task at all, or otherwise they may spend a disproportionate amount of time and energy on it, as they feel they are in competition with someone else. They may even do it half-heartedly, secure in the knowledge that someone else is covering them if they get poor results.

What exactly do you want done?

Ask yourself exactly what the parameters for the task or project are. *

Time spent now in defining the job will make things a lot simpler in the long run.

* Don't abdicate – set limits and stick to them.

~ What task?

~ To what standard?

~ By when?

~ How accurately?

~ How will you judge or measure results?

~ What are the constraints:
Time?
Money?
Resources?
People?

~ How much autonomy can you let them
have?

~ What do you need reporting back on, and
by when?

Identify candidates

Deciding who to delegate to can be difficult.
But then, most people never actually sit
down and make a logically thought-out
decision – they just see who is free or can do
the work already, and delegate to them. *

** If you want
something done,
ask a busy person
- unless you want
to delegate
properly!*

So the exercise of simply taking the time to
look at everyone's skills and experience can

show you new delegation opportunities you hadn't even thought of!

Know people

~ Find out their skills, abilities, experience and interests.

~ An audit is a useful exercise – you will probably find that almost everyone has skills you never even knew about.

~ Don't ignore people's interests.

~ A person who is keen to learn something is worth several who do a task because they have to.

Think about your options

~ Do they have the time to do the task? It's pointless trying to delegate if someone is already overloaded.

~ Do they have the ability? Can they already do the task?

~ Can you train/coach them? If people don't have the experience or skill, but the ability

– the future potential to learn how to do this task – you can delegate to them with training/coaching/support.

~ Would they enjoy it? There's no rule that you can't give awful jobs to someone, but if you try to match up interests and likes with delegation, you will have happier, more willing people around you.

Planning

Now you can plan how to delegate the task.

Before you delegate

~ Do they understand the objectives of the task?

~ Do they have the skills or potential to do the job?

~ Has anyone else done this job before, so that they can seek guidance?

~ Do you know their strengths and weaknesses?

~ Are you confident that they will succeed?

~ Are they confident about this type of work?

~ Will they want to do it, or will they need persuasion?

~ Will the task fit comfortably into their schedule/workload?

~ Can you trust them? If not, you'll spend more time constantly checking up on them than you would have spent on the task itself!

~ Will they follow procedures?

~ Will they learn from the experience?

~ Will this benefit you, them or someone else? *

Avoiding dumping

~ Balance tedious or difficult tasks between people.

~ Be fair in sharing out tasks that are:
   - interesting
   - enjoyable
   - or will gain the person recognition.

Try to address problems before they occur – it will save you time and effort, even unpleasantness in the long run.

~ Keep some rotten jobs for yourself – to be seen to be fair!

~ Ask people what tasks they like and dislike – never assume.

Responsibility, accountability and authority

Giving a task to someone is not effective delegation. To develop, people need some measure of authority to make decisions. It is helpful to bear in mind:

~ responsibility
~ authority
~ and accountability

as these will help you to remember how to view delegation.

Responsibility

Responsibility is not something you can actually give to a person. It is something that has to be taken by them. A common problem with delegation is giving someone a job and giving them responsibility for it. Of course, if that person doesn't accept responsibility for it, if they still think of it as your task, things can go very wrong.

Accountability

Accountability is what you do delegate. You make the person accountable to you for the task, but you yourself remain responsible for the outcome – even though you have delegated it. *

Authority

Authority is power over something. Giving someone the authority to carry out a task, and not publicising the fact to others will make things very difficult. You need to brief others that someone has your authority regarding this task, and that they should co-operate with them as they would with you. If people have insufficient authority, they may feel unable to make decisions without referring back to you, even unable to act at all.

Make someone accountable for the task, but keep responsibility for it yourself.

Balancing the three

The best delegation relies on giving someone the appropriate amount of authority, and publicising this to everyone associated with the task. You make them accountable to you for the task. But the real responsibility for the task remains with you. After all, it's your task, and part of your job. *

So don't shirk your responsibility. If things go wrong it's no use saying, 'I gave you responsibility for this, it's your fault!' It's actually yours. Remember you can't give away responsibility and you won't go far wrong.

The beauty of thinking this way is that you can't steal someone's limelight. If you've publicised that someone else is authorised to do the task, and then if they do a particularly good job, people will know that person did it and not you. Poor managers often steal the credit for something they haven't done, which is bad management and very demotivating.

* *Keep responsibility but give them as much authority as they need. It makes it safe for them to fail, which takes the pressure off – they may even do a better job as a result.*

Summary points

★ Never delegate without giving sensible thought to the task. Is it fair and proper to delegate this task?

★ Set parameters and define exactly what you want to delegate and how. If you don't know what you want, the chances are that you won't get it.

★ Identify the candidates for delegation, and match people to tasks sensibly. Stretching someone is one thing, but make sure that they are capable of the task, after training and support if necessary.

★ Plan what you're delegating, and avoid dumping on people.

★ Give authority, keep the responsibility for the task, and make people accountable to you.

3 Handling People

You can be brilliant at delegation in theory, but things will still go very wrong unless you know how to deal with people effectively.

In this chapter, five things that really matter:

~ **Sound people out**

~ **Gain co-operation and agreement**

~ **Handle difficulties**

~ **Develop people**

~ **Publicise and inform**

You need to consider people and their feelings when delegating, as people will make or break a task or project. People's feelings can be more important than their skills in doing a task, and behaviour and feelings can rub off onto others.

You also need to think not just about the person you are delegating to, but about the people around them. Positive feelings such as motivation, competition, support and admiration can be generated, but so can negative ones such as jealousy, envy, resentment etc.

Delegating properly requires you to think about these things beforehand. How will the person you are delegating to react? How will others perceive the delegation? Will any problems result? Can you avoid these before they occur?*

Is this you?

Look, these people work for me. It's not as if they're going to say 'no', is it? • I hate asking them to do *anything*, let alone part of my own job! • Why does delegation always end up upsetting someone, or producing some kind of unpleasantness? • My people are pretty good at what they do. I can delegate anything to them with confidence. • It takes so long going through everything and answering all the questions and worries, I might just as well do it myself!

* People and their attitudes are paramount in delegating successfully, or you can create difficulties that will last for some time to come.

Sound people out

Before you make the decision to delegate anything, it makes sense to sound people out. If you don't actually check people's availability and ability, you could be making assumptions about how easy it will be to delegate. Jumping to conclusions about people usually causes problems.

Workload

Always check how busy people are – if they seem very quiet, they could be waiting for another substantial task to start, and delegating to them would overload them. Conversely, people who seem busy may be filling in time because they don't want to appear lazy.

Ability

Check that people are able to take on the task. Just because you know they can doesn't mean they feel they can. You may need to bolster their confidence a little, so that they also have faith in their ability.

Willingness

Asking for volunteers often yields surprising results – you may even be lucky enough to find the person you want to do the task volunteering! This lets you delegate to them with their permission and agreement, and their motivation will be that much better. You might also find that someone you had judged unlikely to be interested in the job volunteers. *

Gain co-operation and agreement

It is almost impossible to delegate successfully to someone without their co-operation and consent. Of course you can just make them do the task, if you are their manager or supervisor, but the consequences of this can be very bad for the workplace as a whole. It is far better to sell a task to someone, and gain their co-operation and agreement.

* Never make assumptions about people. There is no substitute for getting your information first-hand.

Lack of agreement

Unless you gain people's agreement to a task, things can go very wrong:

~ They usually don't take responsibility for the task.

~ They often complain to others, and morale and atmosphere decline.

~ They may do a poor job, so you won't ask them again.

~ They could do the job barely adequately; results are mediocre.

~ They will sometimes leave things until the last minute (procrastination) and then can't get it done in time.

~ There's a bad atmosphere between you as a result.

~ They don't do the task properly, so you have to re-do it anyway.

~ They keep running to you with constant questions and issues, causing endless interruptions.

How to gain agreement

~ Ask for volunteers.

~ Ask for help. Human nature is usually to be helpful, so if you take an approach asking for help, it often gets the result you desire: 'I've got a problem, and I wondered if you would be prepared to help me with…' Most people will respond with a yes, and agree to the delegation.

~ Explain the benefits – for them, for you and for everyone concerned.

~ Establish their worth. Flattery is insincere, but sincere praise for past jobs and recognition of their talents can put someone in a positive frame of mind, and more likely to agree to what you ask.

~ Ask, don't tell. If they say no, then you can always fall back on telling them. *

* People working on a task they have agreed to do will always be more motivated and committed than people press-ganged into it.

Never

~ bribe
~ threaten (it's blackmail!)
~ bargain

~ offer rewards (it's bribery)
~ be dishonest
~ fool them into saying yes
~ make them feel guilty about saying no
~ forget to thank people for agreeing.

Handle difficulties

Difficulties can arise from two causes:

1 The person accepts the delegation but makes it clear that they aren't happy about it (grudging acceptance).

2 They refuse.

Grudging acceptance

You need to think about this carefully. Do you really want them to do the job, knowing that it will cause an unpleasant atmosphere, even tension between you? The alternative is to back off and give the task to someone else. However that can make you appear weak as a manager or supervisor. It can even encourage people to use this tactic again, so that you end up being dictated to by your staff if you aren't careful how you handle this problem.

In any event, you need to be very careful as to how you handle the situation. You are caught between being dictatorial on the one hand, and on the other, being a pushover.

You could always confront the issue. Say 'I can sense a reluctance on your part to take this on. I don't want to cause you any problems, so can I ask what's behind that?'

You could always give someone a choice between the task they're reluctant to take on, and something else.

Saying no

If they refuse the task, you must check their reasons. Ask them directly why they don't want to do it, and address their concerns. Maybe they feel unable to manage it, or are concerned that they won't have time. Once you know their reasons, you can deal with them and often they will end up being happy to accept the job.

You can handle objections by playing 'What if…'. If time is the issue, for example, address this by saying 'What if I moved some of your routine work so you had time to do this?' If confidence is the issue, 'What if I told you that I chose you specifically for this task because I know you can do a thorough job and that's what I need right now?' *

Develop people

Develop people by delegating to them. This boost to their skills, experience and career prospects can be very motivating for people, and everyone likes to feel that they are making progress. You can also develop people in your team for the long-term, so that you can delegate more to them in the future.

~ Encourage people to be proactive about discussing what tasks or projects they would like to be involved with.

~ Delegate high-visibility tasks that get people noticed, in order to give them career opportunities.

* *Handling objections is difficult. But the alternative is backing down, and possibly not getting the job done. Don't set yourself up for future difficulty by letting people dictate to you.*

~ Develop yourself – delegation is a learning exercise for you, as well as for the other person.

~ Develop people's trust and confidence in yourself, by delegating well and providing ongoing support and encouragement – without taking over.

~ Delegate whole tasks or projects wherever possible, so that people can get a better sense of how processes work.

~ Explain how the delegation will help them progress. *

Publicise and inform

Earlier we looked at responsibility, accountability and authority. Giving someone authority has to be publicised. If people don't know that you've given a task to someone, they may not give that person their support and co-operation. It may even make it impossible for the person to get the task done. More likely, it will make them look silly. Not informing people about a

Always remember to tell people what's in it for them.

delegated task is quite likely to lead to humiliation for the person concerned, and they will feel negatively about the whole process.

Tell those involved

Tell everyone involved with the task or project. Make sure that they know the extent of the person's authority, so they can give the help and support that will be needed.

Tell colleagues

Tell their colleagues, even if they aren't involved with the task. That way, everyone knows they are working on a special task for you. People will be made aware that you pass work on, and you may get volunteers for other tasks. It's motivating to see others get on, generally speaking, so overall the atmosphere should be positive. It also avoids anyone feeling left out. *

* Let people know what's going on. It's demotivating to keep people in the dark, plus problems can result.

Tell superiors

Tell your own manager or supervisor that you've delegated a task. That way, if you are not around, the person doing the task has a last resort to go to for help or guidance. Plus, it allows the person to be seen to have done the task, and they get to receive the credit for their own work.

Summary points

★ Before you start delegating, sound people out about it – you may be surprised at what you learn.

★ Make sure you gain agreement. Grudging co-operation can be worse than none at all.

★ If people refuse a task, you need to handle things carefully in order to avoid being seen to be weak and ineffectual.

★ Make sure that people learn from delegation, and they will be motivated.

★ Publicise the delegation, so that credit is given where it is due, and so that people co-operate where necessary without checking with you.

4 The Delegation Meeting

Getting together with someone in order to delegate needn't necessarily be a formal meeting, but you do need to make sure you deal with everything, to avoid problems before they even arise.

In this chapter, five things that really matter:

~ **Set the scene**

~ **Standards, progress, deadlines and objectives**

~ **Objective-setting**

~ **Set limits – the big picture**

~ **Confirm and check**

When you delegate, you must brief the person who will be doing the task or project. This is the delegation meeting. It is your opportunity to make sure that all goes smoothly later.

Use the meeting wisely, and you can prevent problems from arising and establish an effective relationship for the duration of the project or task. Handle the meeting badly, and the person may leave feeling resentful, put upon, confused and swamped by a task which they feel is way beyond their abilities.

A little thought given to the structure of the meeting will ensure that the person receives everything they need to continue and carry out the task successfully. They should leave feeling motivated and confident. You should feel confident, and not concerned that won't they succeed. *

Is this you?

I've always just let people get on and handle things their own way. • Simple tasks don't need briefing sessions – there's not much that can go wrong anyway. • If anyone needs help they'll shout , so what's the worry? • People can ask me if they need to know anything. Otherwise, let them get on with it.

* You should be secure in the knowledge that they will only come to you if necessary.

Set the scene

At the very start you need to let the person know why you are delegating to them.

Remember, things are always more effective if you point out what's in it for them. Brief them in general terms:

~ how the task arose
~ what needs doing
~ why it needs doing
~ why you chose them to delegate it to
~ what's in it for them.

Sometimes it can be useful to give people a little bit of the background and history to a task or project, so that they see the whole picture. *

Standards, progress, deadlines and objectives

If you don't define precisely what has to be done, to what standard, and by when, you aren't likely to get a successful result from your delegation. People aren't mindreaders – you actually need to spell things out for them. You'd never ask a builder to just put up a wall – you'd specify what, how, when, what materials, desired result, timescales etc.

* *Start off like anything else – with an introduction.*

Standards

~ Specify the desired outcome – exactly
  what needs doing. *

~ Specify the exact standard(s) you require.

~ Set goals and objectives.

~ Specify the consequences of not achieving
  the desired standard. It can put people's
  minds at rest if they don't have the
  constant worry that failure will have
  serious consequences.

Progress

~ Establish regular sessions to get progress
  reports. The urge to ask how things are
  going too often is removed if you plan
  regular updates, and this makes the
  person feel less as if you are watching
  them all the time.

~ Establish a process for major problems or
  difficulties. It's helpful to agree a time
  period for which they can struggle with
  the problem before they must alert you to
  the situation.

** If you don't know
exactly what you
want, you won't
get it – even if the
other person is
psychic!*

Deadlines

~ Always establish deadlines for the end result.

~ Also consider setting interim objectives – i.e. progress which should be achieved by a certain date. This enables you to be sure that things are on track. *

Objective-setting

Setting objectives is not nearly as simple a task as most people think.   Good objectives do four things:

~ They show what to work towards.

~ They give a means to measure achievement.

~ They motivate people, as people are motivated by achievement and recognition.

~ They prevent wasted effort.

* Objective setting is not a waste of time. It is the single thing most likely to gain successful outcomes.

Follow these rules for successful outcomes:

~ **Agree** objectives jointly – people will almost always be more committed if they agree to something.

~ **Specific** objectives will make it easier to see whether they have been achieved.

~ **Measurable** outcomes are necessary – if an objective cannot be measured, you certainly can't assess whether it has been achieved or not.

~ **Timescales** have to be set. Otherwise the job may take longer than you had imagined, or even never get done.

~ **Realistic** objectives may stretch people, but they are achievable. Unrealistic objectives are very demotivating. You need to make sure that objectives set are actually within the capabilities of the person.

~ **Method** of achieving the objective should be left up to the person doing the task, if at all possible. This is how you can give people the freedom to learn for themselves, which is often a process that teaches them by trial and error.

~ **Develop** people by setting them objectives that stretch them.

~ **Review** progress regularly.

~ **Clarity** of objectives is essential. As you can see below, clear or unclear objectives will have different effects upon the person to whom you are delegating.

	Vague about the circumstances/ background	*Clear about the circumstances/ background*
Clear about the task	FRUSTRATION Can do the task, but no sense of why, or where it fits in	OPTIMUM PERFORMANCE Can do the job to the best of their ability
Vague about the task	CONFUSION No idea what to do or why – muddling along	DISILLUSIONMENT Knows the background and appreciates the need, but doesn't know what to do about it

Set limits – the big picture

It helps the person you are delegating to enormously if they understand the limits surrounding the task. Let people know the 'big picture', so that they can see exactly where their work fits in.

Wider aims and objectives

If the person being delegated to appreciates the overall place of the task in the grand scheme of things, they are far more likely to understand how the job needs to be done. It will also increase their job satisfaction.

Resources and support

All the physical resources needed to complete the task must be made available. You may also need to give help and/or guidance in how to identify and obtain the necessary resources. You may also need to check the availability of resources before setting the task.

Support is, after all, a resource. You need to reassure the person of what support is available to them. Then make it clear to anyone supposed to give support that they need to make it available. Just setting a follow-up time can give support, as the person you are delegating to knows when they will next have your undivided attention.

If necessary, formally allocate people to give support and assistance, especially if you will be unavailable whilst the task is in progress for any reason.

Communication

Communicating to others that you have delegated this particular task is a vital part of setting limits. Unless you do this, people will not be aware that the person doing the task has the authority to take action and to do things which they would not normally be doing.

Responsibility and accountability

When you delegate, remember that you are making the person accountable to you. But the responsibility for the task remains firmly on your own shoulders. You cannot delegate responsibility – if the person chooses to take on responsibility, great, but it doesn't remove your own. You set the task, so *you* are responsible for it. So if it goes wrong, you take the consequences.

Levels of authority

There are several levels of authority you can delegate to someone, ranging from giving them very much a free hand, to keeping a high level of control over the task. If the person taking on the task is not absolutely certain how much authority they have to make decisions and act on them, things can go very wrong indeed. So it's vital that there are no misunderstandings surrounding how much control you are retaining: *

* Make sure everyone knows the limits to their actions and decisions. Otherwise, misunderstandings can easily turn into catastrophes, before the problem is even detected.

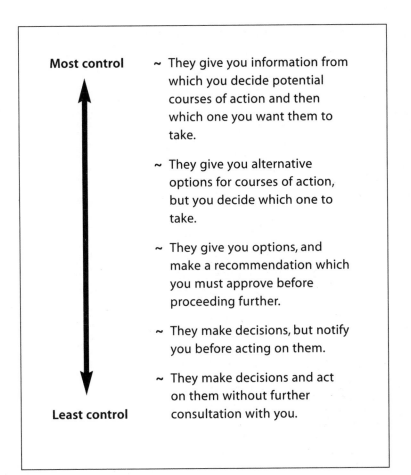

Most control

~ They give you information from which you decide potential courses of action and then which one you want them to take.

~ They give you alternative options for courses of action, but you decide which one to take.

~ They give you options, and make a recommendation which you must approve before proceeding further.

~ They make decisions, but notify you before acting on them.

~ They make decisions and act on them without further consultation with you.

Least control

Confirm and check

As a final point, never assume that after the meeting (or any meeting for that matter) the other person's understanding of what was said matches your own. Check that they understand you correctly. It can be useful either to ask a few questions to check they understand, or to get them to summarise things for you. *

This may sound a little bit demeaning to the other person, but if approached in a friendly manner it hopefully won't look as though you think they are a complete idiot! Say something like:

'Let's just check we both understand this…'

'So if I've got this correct, you're going to do things in this order…'

'Okay, just to make sure I've made myself clear, can you summarise for me?'

'I know there's a lot to take in. Why don't you run through your understanding for me, so that I can make sure you've got all the information you need.'

* *What you think you said isn't always what you actually did say – or what they think you said. Or what you actually meant…*

Summary points

★ Set the scene, and give the person an awareness of where the task fits in.

★ Setting standards in your own mind makes it easy to brief others.

★ Setting good, clear objectives gives clear guidance and measures of success.

★ Make people's limits of authority absolutely clear.

★ Always check that there have been no misunderstandings – assumptions can be very dangerous.

5 Keeping Your Distance

You can't simply delegate a task to somebody and walk off into the sunset – you need to keep your distance, but also be available for help and support when needed.

In this chapter, four things that really matter:

~ **Give support and coaching**
~ **Keep control and distance**
~ **Monitor progress**
~ **Corrective action**

One of the hardest things about delegation is the delicate balance between constantly watching over someone, and walking away from a task leaving the person to sink or swim.

Being watched or fussed over is a nightmare for someone trying to do a task to the best of their ability – and rarely produces a person's best performance. But the pressure of being left to your own devices can also cause a lot of anxiety, so this balance is very important.

Keeping your distance is actually a very difficult skill to master. Too much distance, and you leave the person feeling abandoned. Too little, and they feel under constant scrutiny. Getting it just right means that you are there and able to help when needed, but are otherwise able to give the person a free hand. *

Is this you?

You don't seriously expect me to sit back and do nothing, do you? • What if they mess up? • I've told them everything I know – surely it's up to them to just get on with it? • I figure they know where I am if they need me – they don't want me looking over their shoulder all the time. • I thought I ought to check up on people regularly, just ask how they're doing, that sort of thing…

* If they aren't allowed to make a mistake, they aren't ever really going to learn effectively.

Give support and coaching

It may be that a person you want to delegate to needs help with how to do things. There are various ways of handling this. Giving support is being available for advice and discussion; teaching is giving someone information, whereas coaching is talking through an issue, or training of some sort.

If the task requires training or coaching, you need to agree with the person about how this will take place, by what deadline etc. You may need to set up a schedule of sessions to formalise things, because otherwise informal coaching sessions have a habit of being rescheduled and never end up actually taking place.

You also need to agree a date for completion of any training or coaching. On this date you should both review progress, and see whether they now have the skills necessary to do the task. If not, you need to look at other options.

The importance of coaching

If you do need to do any coaching or training, always make sure that you arrange this at a quiet time, and give it the attention it deserves. It is most unfair to skimp on such sessions, or the person who is left with the task may do a less than adequate job. This won't just affect the task results, it may ultimately affect the person's confidence and their willingness to take on tasks again. *

Demonstrations

Give demonstrations where possible, rather than factual explanations and descriptions. The best method is to actually go through with them the part of the task with which they need help.

Keep control and distance

Sometimes the temptation to step in and check up on people, to lend a hand, or even take over, can be overwhelming. Keeping control from a healthy distance is essential. You need to keep a measure of control for your own peace of mind, but you should also keep sufficient distance that the other person can feel relaxed.

Actually, what you really need is sufficient confidence in the other person to be able to

* If people need support and/or coaching, make sure you make time available for them. The time spent doing this will be recovered later when they can act on their own.

relax and let them get on with the job. That only comes with time – it is highly unlikely that you will feel confident they can do a new task the first time they attempt it, especially if it is demanding for them. But once you know that they can work on their own to a sufficient standard, you need to learn to trust them and relax.

Concern vs. freedom

There is nothing wrong with feeling concerned that the task is done properly. In fact you should, because that is part of keeping overall responsibility for the task. But the person with the task needs the freedom to do it in their own way, to make mistakes, to find out how best they can do it – which is part of their own learning process. *

If you trust them to do the job in the first place, you have to trust them to get on with it without constant supervision.

Monitoring progress can be the perfect way to have enough feedback to put your mind at rest.

Monitor progress

You need to have a way of monitoring progress so that you can step back and let the person do the task on their own. Otherwise, you have no way of knowing whether or not you should be confident that they are coping. Monitoring progress by constantly asking if people are all right is not very helpful. It may make them feel you don't trust them, or that you don't think they are capable of carrying out the task.

Regular feedback

Regular feedback is a good way to set your mind at rest about progress without over-involvement. Feedback can be obtained at regular meetings, catch-up sessions, or by reports or notes. A daily email update on progress can work well for small tasks.

It is better to schedule feedback than to ask for it on an ad-hoc basis. Of course, you need to make it clear that if matters are urgent, for example if they can't proceed without consulting you, or there is a major problem, they can come to you outside of the planned time. But for routine feedback and questions, plan times when you will be available, so that they can report back. *

Advantages for you

~ It puts your mind at rest.

~ You know how things are progressing.

~ You are less likely to be interrupted with queries and/or feedback about the task.

~ It helps you resist the temptation to interfere.

Advantages for the other person:

~ They can find it very useful to have to think through the task at regular intervals in order to brief you. This is especially true if the task is long or complex.

~ They know when they will have your attention to raise problems, questions, etc.

~ If they have any doubts, problems or questions, they can keep these until the next feedback session, instead of having to disturb you with them.

Regular feedback is helpful and reassuring for both parties. But never forget to make it clear that emergencies or major issues can be brought to you outside of the regular feedback schedule.

~ They needn't feel concerned or foolish about coming to you.

~ Potential problems can be nipped in the bud before they get to a stage where they cause difficulties.

Corrective action

It is especially tempting to think of intervening (or even taking over) if you can see that things are starting to go wrong. But you must try to avoid this at all costs. Your preferred actions should always be (in this order):

1 Let them continue the task with increased help, support and/or supervision.

2 Step in and do the task with them.

3 Take over the task.

4 Give the task to someone else (always the last resort).

If things go wrong

Wait

If you can wait a little before the problem becomes catastrophic, schedule a catch-up session and then get the problem out into the open. Then you can offer help and advice.

Give them the opportunity to tell you

Either at the catch-up session, or if you need to step in immediately, try simply asking how things are going. This gives the person the opportunity to admit that there is a problem and to ask for help, without letting them know you have noticed anything amiss. You only need to step in if they don't admit or see that there is a problem.

Keep things between yourselves

If you do need to step in, do it confidentially. Ask for a briefing, and in private, try not to tell them you have noticed anything wrong – try asking questions in order to get them to realise what is happening and raise the problem themselves.

Taking over

There will inevitably come a point where a task goes so badly wrong that you just want to take it away from the person and do it yourself, or give it to someone else. This is never a good idea, however.

Giving a task to someone else is a public advertisement that the person has failed; that they are less capable than the new person given the task. It will cause humiliation and ill-feeling. The person affected may lose all their confidence, or become the subject of gossip or workplace jokes.

If it really is necessary, take back the task and do it yourself – but try to avoid this becoming public knowledge. This saves face for the person concerned, gets the task done, and you have learnt what they are not capable of doing. They have learned what not to do, and hopefully will be more aware of their own limits. These solutions are never as good as letting them continue with increased help and support, however. *

* Intervening in a task you've delegated is a tricky thing to do, and needs great care if you aren't going to shake the person's self-confidence, or humiliate them in front of others.

Reassure people

Always reassure people if things have gone wrong. No one likes to feel there's a black cloud hovering over them, so be honest about performance and problems, and then move on. Build the person's confidence again, too, or they may find it difficult to keep motivated in future.

It is an excellent idea if there has been a failure to get a task done to delegate something else to them quite soon. This gives people a chance to achieve, and put things behind them. It also gives them something to do so that they don't dwell on their mistakes. Finally, it prevents people from speculating about their performance – if you trust them to do another task, they know where they stand a lot better.

Summary points

★ Make sure people have (or are learning) the skills and support they need to do the task.

★ Staying out of the way and resisting the temptation to watch over people can be hard, but you have to try to relax and let them get on with it.

★ Schedule regular feedback to monitor progress.

★ When things go wrong, think very carefully about how to retrieve the situation.

6 Getting Results and Action

To get consistently good results with your delegation, you need to take some follow-up action between tasks.

In this chapter, four things that really matter:

~ **Evaluate success**

~ **Keep records**

~ **Move forward**

~ **Towards an ideal situation**

After the task has been completed you need to evaluate the success, so that you can plan for future delegation. Each task you delegate is not just an isolated incident which is forgotten about when it's over. You should be planning to make some tasks permanently the responsibility of others, if things work out well.

Over a period of time, planning and monitoring can help you develop other people's skills and experience by delegating to them regularly. It can make sure that after delegating a task, the person doesn't just take it on and then stop learning and growing in experience.

Delegation is a powerful management tool, but to use it effectively, it needs planning and evaluation. *

Is this you?

Don't ask me! I used to do that, but now I've delegated it to Simon – it's his baby now. • Hey, what a great thought! Everyone else can do all the tasks we have to cover, and I'll just manage them doing them. • Delegating a task is all very well, but what happens afterwards – they'll only have a backlog of their own work! • If I share out all my own work, what will I do all day? • Delegating the odd thing now and then is one thing, but handing over large parts of your job? I'd be nervous about that.

* A good programme of planned delegation can form the basis for keeping people challenged and motivated, as well as providing valuable contingency resources for when people are absent.

Evaluate success

After a task is over, it's tempting to just leave things at that – especially if the task either went perfectly, or really badly! Each delegated task isn't an isolated incident, however, and so you really owe it to the other person to evaluate the delegation, and then sit down with them and discuss it.

Evaluate results not methods

To a certain extent, the end justifies the means in delegation. If the person has achieved the results you wanted, but by using their own methods, what difference does it make? If their method is slower than your own, let them find this out for themselves. Unless the methods they used have caused a real problem, they aren't relevant. What you can (and should) do is to try to get the person to see if their methods have been particularly time consuming, or inefficient, for example. But at the end of the day, if the results are good, they deserve credit and it should be given. Let them work in their own way wherever possible.

Reasons for failure

Failure or problems need to be analysed. You need to reassure the person that you are interested in *why* things went wrong, not the details of what happened. The fact that they made a mistake is not the issue – but the fact that they have learned what not to do next time is.

Reward and achievement

You need to remember to praise people for good work. Good work can include good effort which failed just short of getting the desired result, as well as actually achieving good results. People get a sense of achievement from knowing you value what they have done, so tell them.

Praising effort

So what about if they have not managed to get the task done correctly, but gave it their best attempt? Well, telling someone you like the way they did something does not detract from the fact that they may have failed to get the right result. You can praise their effort, even if the results were not as expected.

On the other hand, telling them you love the result they achieved does not detract from the fact that they may have got there in a very long-winded way. You would need to discuss this with them as well.

The best rule of thumb is to praise the success they have had, then discuss things from which they could learn and improve. *

Constructive feedback

Giving feedback consisting of advice and support to rectify mistakes and shortcomings is constructive. It enables learning. Pointing out mistakes and shortcomings, without offering any suggestion for how to remedy them is not constructive at all.

The best way to give feedback is in a sandwich! Find something good you can mention, then discuss the problems, difficulties or lack of performance. Then end with some praise for some aspect of the task they did well. This sandwich of positive–negative–positive feedback will make the bad news easier to accept.

* Evaluate the success and praise it. Then discuss the less-successful or unsuccessful aspects of the performance under review.

Packaging the negative feedback between some positives lets people process the negative feedback without becoming upset, defensive, hurt etc. It salves their feelings, whilst still getting the points across.

Keep records

Most organisations have some kind of appraisal or performance review system. This means that people are assessed at regular intervals, usually once a year for example.

Keeping records of delegation means that you can give credit where it's due. All too often we leave evaluating people until that once-a-year occasion when we have to. But setting targets and objectives throughout the year for people is a far better way to manage them.

If nothing else, it can be very valuable to record who in your team can do what, in case of an emergency. That way, if someone unexpectedly falls ill, you know who can step in to continue and pick up certain parts of their work. If you yourself are away from work for any period of time unexpectedly, records can enable people to see who can pick up what tasks, to keep things going in your absence.

A clear picture of who you have delegated tasks to can avoid confusion, as well. People feel that they are progressing, career-wise, if they know they are learning how to do new tasks. *

Move forward

What happens next?

After delegation, what happens next? Will that person continue to do that task now? Will they go on and learn more new skills by having other tasks delegated to them?

You need to think about these issues, because delegation often raises expectations. People tend to think after they have learned how to do new work that they are progressing. This may raise expectations of career advancement, or even simply that they will be given more responsibility on a regular basis. You need to think about how

* Don't fail to record delegation, especially if it was very successful. People are entitled to recognition for what they have done.

to deal with raised expectations, if they
occur.

One-off projects

If your delegation is a one-off project, which
helps you out in a tight spot, there may be
limited opportunities for other delegation. It
could be that you haven't really any other
tasks that would be appropriate for
delegating.

If this is so, people need to be told. A one-
off delegation which is never repeated may
well lead people to assume that something
went wrong if they don't get another chance.
Others may think that they did the task
wrong, and that's why you don't delegate to
the person any more. Avoid
misunderstandings by making it clear when
delegating one-off projects that this is all
they are.

Ongoing processes

Delegation is an ongoing process. It keeps
the workflow changing, and provides
challenge and motivation. People should be

encouraged to ask about new things they could take on. It could well be that someone will volunteer to do a task for you that you hadn't thought of when you were looking at tasks that could be delegated.

Don't keep all the nice jobs!

Take a long, hard look at your work. What should you be delegating – as opposed to what are you happy to delegate? You can't keep all the nice jobs to yourself. You should certainly keep some tasks which you enjoy doing, so that your own job keeps you motivated. But don't hang on to all the nice tasks and delegate the rest – it's unfair, and people will see this and resent the tasks you do delegate.

Be fair and firm

Don't leave people out, and don't overload one good person. If you don't want to delegate to someone, tell them why (if you can without hurting their feelings). Try to spread your delegation evenly, so that everyone feels they have the chance to learn new tasks, progress their careers and improve their skills. *

Towards an ideal situation

Delegation is one of the most effective management tools at your disposal. It enables you to enjoy many advantages, and the sheer act of delegating in itself teaches you a vital management skill. Delegation means that you have to evaluate what you do and the way you do it, which is almost always a good thing.

Delegating also means that you have to deal with people professionally and sensitively. Your communication skills will be tested, practised and developed. In short, your own management skills will be improved by your delegating to others, as well as saving you time!

Delegation enables you to:

You don't just delegate a task and that's it – delegation is an ongoing process.

~ Give people authority and accountability, not just work and tasks.

~ Give people the opportunity to take on

responsibility.

~ Make people feel their suggestions and input are valued.

~ Stretch people by taking their capabilities a little further than normal.

~ Motivate people by varying their work.

~ Let people learn from their own mistakes.

Good delegation shows you are a good manager. If you were ill for a few days, and your staff could manage to get everything done without you, it doesn't mean you aren't needed – it shows what an effective team you have built. *

* *Having an effective team is one of the best measures of a successful manager. Delegation is one of the best ways to create an effective team.*

Summary points

★ Evaluate results and success of the delegation when it is over.

★ Keep a record – people deserve the credit for things they do.

★ Plan, and keep the momentum going so that people continue to progress.

★ Use delegation as an effective management tool.